It's Cool to...
Listen To Teachers

The Confident Ummah

Copyright © 2022

All rights reserved. Without limiting rights under the copyright reserved above, no part of this publication may be reproduced, stored, introduced into a retrieval system, distributed or transmitted in any form or by any means, including without limitation photocopying, recording, or other electronic or mechanical methods, without the prior written permission of the publisher, except in the case of brief quotations embodied in critical reviews and certain other non-commercial uses permitted by copyright law.

The scanning, uploading, and/or distribution of this document via the internet or via any other means without the permission of the publisher is illegal and is punishable by law. Please purchase only authorized editions and do not participate in or encourage electronic piracy of copyrightable materials

About the Author

Welcome to The Confident Ummah, Adab Series. We were inspired to create books for our children and ummah so they can refer to them throughout their early years and better themselves as Muslims.

The first 10 years of a child's life are the most impressionable. This is when their foundations are formed and so it is the best time to encourage positive traits, so they are equipped with the tools to live healthy and balanced lives through which they worship and serve Allah ﷻ.

Each storybook has been designed to focus on a main principle, followed by related Qur'an/Hadith quotes. The moral of the story section highlights the core lessons from the storybook. Finally, we have included an activity page which is designed to encourage your child to implement the story's lessons.

Our stories are based on questions our children ask us and scenarios we have come across in our daily lives whilst homeschooling them.

We ask Allah ﷻ to accept our efforts in spreading useful knowledge and to strengthen (and unite) our ummah. Ameen.

Bismillahir Rahmanir Raheem

In the name of Allah, the Most Beneficent, the Most Merciful

It was Tuesday morning and the children were excited for their classes. After breakfast, their mother reminds them to say Alhamdulillah.

Alhamdulillah - All Praise Be To Allah

"Remember to sit when drinking water. It's Sunnah to drink this way, which means it's also good for us," says their mother.

"Jazak'Allah Khairun for the reminders mummy," says Taiba.

"Yes my darling. It is important that we always learn and apply new life lessons. We want to be the best Muslims we can be," says her mother.

Jazak'Allah Khairun - May Allah be pleased with you

They set off for their sports class excited to see everyone. They run across the park towards their teacher.
"COACH KHADRA!" They shout excitedly.

"Assalamauliakum little ones, I've missed you all so much." Says coach Khadra. Their friends Saad, Isaa and Nour also arrive.

Assalamaulaikum - Peace & Blessings be on you

Malaika and Saba laid out the cones neatly. Nour then started to throw them everywhere.
"Please stop," asks coach Khadra nicely. But Nour continued.

One of the cones accidently hits Yahya on the head.
"Nour, this could have been avoided if you listened to me straight away," says coach Khadra.
"I'm so sorry! It will not happen again," replies Nour.

Their class starts. Their first game is called Fruit Hoops. The coach has to shout a fruit and you have to run to the matching coloured hoop.

"Strawberries!" She shouts. They run to the red hoop.

"Blueberries!" They all run to the blue hoop.

"Watermelons!" Everyone looks confused.
"Run to green!" Shouts Haaniya.
"But watermelons are red," replies Malaika.
"And they have black seeds," says 'Isaa. They all laugh!

The children played different games for the hour.
"Well done children, I was very impressed with how well you listened today. Come and collect the stickers you've earned."
Even baby Zaynab recieved two little stickers on her cheeks.

Later that day, they had Islamic Studies class. "Assalam'aulaikum," says teacher Shagufta as she greets everyone. The children sit down around her and recite the Qur'an one by one. Faisal recited first. As he was reciting, Humza started to whisper in Umar's ear.

"Shhh please. When someone is reciting Qur'an we must be quiet and listen, we mustn't talk over it. There is plenty of time in the rest of the day to talk to each other," says teacher Shagufta.

After reciting Qur'an the children sit down with teacher Asmaa to learn their weekly Du'a. "Right children, today we will learn a Du'a...." Saba interrupts "I know that Du'a aunty Asmaa."

"No, no, no Saba, we must not talk over a teacher. Our Prophet ﷺ would wait until the person had finished talking before speaking himself," says aunty Asmaa.
"I'm sorry, I was just excited," replies Saba.

"That is okay darling," says aunty Asmaa.
"Right children, the Du'a for looking in the mirror is to ask Allah to make our characteristics just as beautiful as He has made us look." She continues the class with all the children listening carefully.

When aunty Asmaa teaches them, the children sit with their backs up straight, making eye contact. They would then raise their hand if they had a question.

After class, Saba spoke to her father. "Daddy, when I am bigger, I want to be a teacher and also teach in a fun way so that I too can spread knowledge and goodness," she says.

"My children, remember to listen carefully when someone is sharing their knowledge with you. Regardless of their age, we may learn something new from them. We should always be looking for ways to bring us closer to Allah."

Moral of the Story

In this story, we teach our children the importance of listening to people that share valuable knowledge. Children should learn to be attentive towards those that deliver beneficial knowledge about Islam. This will ultimately help us improve our faith and guide us in being closer to Allah, insha'Allah.

The first teacher in this story is their mother. This is because children learn their actions from their parents first and we as parents should do our best to constantly expand our knowledge whilst teaching our children so they have the best chance in life. Personal growth for parents is also crucial as it helps us in being the best parents we can be.

We also cover the topic of how to interact with different types of teachers. Intrigue (asking questions) and respect (listening) being a fundamental part of this.

"So when the Qur'an is recited, then listen to it and pay attention that you may receive mercy" - Qur'an 7:204

"Allah elevates to high positions those from amongst you who are faithful and those who have acquired knowledge" - Quran, 58:11

Abu Umamah Al-Bahuli narrated that Rasoolullah ﷺ said: "Allah ﷻ, His angels, those in heavens and on earth, even the ant in its nest and the fish (all of these) pray for the one who teaches people what is good"

Activity

Look at your schedule of classes for the week. Pick a few that are of interest to you.

The aim is to become inquisitive and learn everything possible about that subject/topic you picked. In order to do this, you will need to pay attention in class and write down any questions you may want to ask. We want you to have everything answered so that you are confident in that topic and are able to explain and teach that concept to others. This would strengthen your understanding.

Listening to teachers is good etiquette and beneficial for ourselves, so its important to show respect by focusing on what is being taught.

This task would be especially beneficial for islamic classes or madrasahs you may be attending as you will be learning islamic knowledge that can help better you as a person, Insha'Allah.

Remember - learning the skill of listening attentively is not a sprint, it's an ongoing marathon.